MAKING UP: POEMS
Copyright © 2020 Respective Writers
All rights reserved. No part of this book may be used or reproduced in any manner whatsoever without written permission from the author, except in the case of credited epigraphs or brief quotations embedded in articles or reviews.

pictureshowpress.net

Cover Art: lekcej, istockphoto.com

FIRST EDITION

ISBN-13: 978-1-7341702-3-8

Making Up

POEMS

Picture Show Press

Contents

1	Ash Wednesday
2	Ashtray
3	At Fourteen I let my *Seventeen* Subscription Lapse
4	Beans
5	Beauty Rituals
8	Because the sky was soft and slow
9	The Book of Snow
10	Cake Face in Four Acts
13	California Snow
14	Chop Suey
15	Cinerama
18	Cold Shoulder
19	Countenance Connotated
20	Cover-up
21	Crossed
23	A Curious Souvenir
25	Dance
26	The Debt
28	Erased by Nostalgia
29	Eyelids
30	For Now
31	Ford Flex
33	Gem-Ignited
34	The Ghost of Stephanie
36	Grief is the thing with fur—
37	"hereditary"
39	I Am
40	if the earth wore mascara
42	In Another Life
43	Learning Make-up

44	Life's Lovely Hit or Miss
46	Lorac Alter Ego: "Secret Agent"
	(Or Other Uses For Lipstick Tubes)
48	The Magician's Assistant
49	Maidens, Made in the Shade
50	Make Believe
51	Makeup
52	Making the Bed
53	Maquillage
54	Maybelline #148: "Summer Pink"
55	Not Your Average Absentee Landlord
57	October
58	Painting of a Female Joker
60	Palette of You
61	Plastic Limbs
62	The Plasticity of Existence
64	The poem about the straight girl who decided I needed a coming out intervention after she kissed me first
65	Poem Without a Name
67	Poem Without the Whole Truth About Sex
68	Portrait of a Sabine Woman
69	A public house is being torn down
73	Reciprocate and Replicate
74	Red Chiffon
76	Revlon #415: "Pink in the Afternoon"
	(Audrey Hepburn's Favorite Shade)
77	Revlon Super Lustrous Lipstick, Crème Color #640, Blackberry: Part I
79	Revlon Super Lustrous Lipstick, Crème Color #640, Blackberry: Part II
80	Saying Things With Our Hands
82	She Died of Her Own Beauty
84	Supernatural Phantom Woman
85	Test

86	The Thing About Love and Flowers
89	This poem is made up
90	Trace
91	Trigger
92	Truth
93	Unforgettable
95	The Warehouse
96	Will you ever stop wanting me?
97	Wrong Number
	(The only question worth asking)
i	CONTENTS
iv	EDITOR'S NOTE
101	*Recommended Reading*
103	ACKNOWLEDGEMENTS
105	BIOS

Editor's Note

I am a nerd for words. Chances are, if you're reading this then you are, too (unless you bought this book in order to support one or more of the poets in it—in which case, even better!).

The idea for this anthology came to me when Suzanne Allen and I were doing a final proofread of her book, *Little Threats*. During the process, we found ourselves looking up how to properly spell makeup—turns out, it's *make up* (the verb) and *makeup* or *make-up* for cosmetics.

For more word-nerd fun, check out Suzanne's experimental piece, *Beauty Rituals*, on page five. Coincidentally, I wrote a creative nonfiction piece on beauty and motherhood, using a very similar format; however, we'd each written our pieces entirely independent of the other. And that is what I love about anthologies like this one—I love to read and see what themes emerge, to get a sense of what overlapping thoughts are collectively occupying us during certain times... or uncertain times...

A cursory perusal of the *Contents* page will reveal three poems with *Revlon* in the title; there are more than a few poems about shoplifting... poems about mothers... poems with snow, thieves... For more, see my recommended reads on p. 101.

Even though cosmetics dominate, there are a handful of poems that deal in the theme of *reconciliation*... Can you find them? Likewise, with the theme of *invention*—though, clearly, the trick is that all poems qualify as invention, don't they?

— Shannon

Ash Wednesday

She lit a fire
in the big black car
to see if the trapeze
swinger could escape
from the trunk.
a forced resurrection
of teeth in the grass
forayed fungi and falcon cries
her makeup smeared
like Ash Wednesday
as she watched the shadows
play with the flames
as the trapeze swinger
popped from the newly crisp
low rider on an idiot wind
with a howl at the moon
dope fiend boogie into the forest
it reminded her of an eight
line poem, an elegy
to the void falling
into place like green onions.

— *Zack Nelson-Lopiccolo*

Ashtray

It looks like a skillet for elves,
this cast-iron ashtray
that once sat next to Father's
big chair and now sits
on the counter, next to my stove.
A stirring spoon rests there.
But one time, as a child,
I left a smoldering pile of stubs
in its cradle. Caught,
I concocted a complex alibi
not yet having learned
the elegant recipe—like
making the crust of a pie,
few ingredients
and don't overwork it—
for a tasty, succulent, lie.

— Donna Hilbert

At Fourteen I Let My *Seventeen* Subscription Lapse

The makeup I stole from Zody's
or Sav-on or one of those stores
since gone, for that fresh-faced look
I longed to emulate.
I'm sure I didn't need to shoplift,
but I needed to take—
to have something I didn't
have to pay for. The cost
of my glycerin eyes
and frosted lips
always too high,
so much at stake.

— Betsy Mars

Beans

Because his mother always
burns the beans
I am careful not to; but once
distracted by the babies at my feet
I let the pot run dry.
Slender fingers of green
ruin to brown with a minute's
inattention, but I refuse defeat
scrape the beans onto his plate
next to meatloaf and mashed potatoes.
He rolls his eyes
and I gather steam, become
the door-to-door salesman of supper:
They are *supposed* to look that way!
Burn-aise sauce, it's *French*, I say.
I saw the recipe on TV, or read it in a book.
Lies tumble from my lips like crumbs
and I invoke the saints of good cuisine:
Julia Child, Betty Crocker, Sara Lee,
so burned to a crisp am I by the thought
of doing wrong and getting caught.

— Donna Hilbert

Beauty Rituals

> *Strong men battle for beautiful women, and beautiful women are more reproductively successful. Women's beauty must correlate to their fertility, and since this system is based on sexual selection, it is inevitable and changeless.*
>
> *None of this is true.*
>
> —Naomi Wolf, *The Beauty Myth*

Usually, I don't do my make-up at my vanity,
but at my mother's writing desk, like she used to,
because I like the way the morning sun falls in through the blinds.

I keep my make-up, the daily stuff, in the right drawer with
envelopes and notepads and mismatched stationary, since I also
use this desk for writing and paper crafts,

> *The problem with cosmetics exists only when women feel invisible or inadequate without them.*

but in the mornings, a silver framed mirror takes the place of my
laptop and craft supplies, and I transform myself.

> *Urban, professional women are devoting up to a third of their income to 'beauty maintenance' and considering it a necessary investment.*

I don't go out without make-up, but when I'm running late, I put
rollers in my hair first. My mother used to roll her hair in plastic
curlers and put one of those big dryer caps over the whole thing, at
least until she discovered the curling iron, but my step-mother
used hot rollers. She sat straddling the toilet seat lid with her
make-up mirror on top of the tank, and I would sit in the doorway

of the bathroom, watching. She sectioned her hair with focus and ease using the pointy end of a teasing brush. To this day, the smell of the hairspray she used reminds me of her.

Like my mother, she was always running late.

> *Whenever we dismiss or do not hear a woman because our attention has been drawn to her size or make-up or clothing or hairstyle, the beauty myth is working with optimum efficiency.*

I'm using a new make-up, something a friend turned me onto, a mineral powder that is strangely reminiscent of a product my mother used in the seventies. I'm addicted to the infomercials:

I do wish this make-up had been around when I was a teenager. I do want a natural foundation that's good for my skin. I do dream of a clearer, healthier looking complexion.

I got my mother's skin.

Growing up, I never thought my mom was pretty, but I knew she had been.

> *...fashion modeling and prostitution are the only professions in which women earn consistently more than men.*

Her career lasted just long enough for her to take some pictures and do a couple of lingerie lunch shows.

She married my dad shortly after that, and when he went to Vietnam, she adopted the nervous habit of picking at her eyebrows. Her naturally full eyebrows, and mine, were a gift from her father. Even as I write this, I have the tweezers and a small mirror within reach.

Every night before bed, my grandma used a "cold cream" that made her face shine and smell like roses. I bought a jar, and every once in a while I scoop a little out to rub into my hands. I pretend I'm sleeping next to her and she's stretched out on her back, snoring.

She never slept with a pillow because it would mess up her hair.

> *Must the expressiveness of maturity*
> *and old age become extinct?*
> *Will we lose nothing if it does?*

What exactly *is* twenty percent of a fine line anyway?

— *Suzanne Allen*

---

*All italicized quotations are from Naomi Wolf's *The Beauty Myth*.

Because the sky was soft and slow

upon waking, she found a smudged
shadow fading, found
it was not hard to turn to the light

and to rise and decide the anger
was no longer welcome
in her house. She forgave

the troubled sleeper behind her.
And so, the rest of her day
was a blouse of silk cascading
down smooth arms—

the rest of her life lit
from behind, a film she
would have enjoyed
seeing again after all.

— Grant Hier

The Book of Snow

Keeps my secrets too.

What winter night I first undressed beneath;

the names of my early poems,
the ones that never left my drawer;

that dream I keep having
where my feet become water,

then stone,
then, finally, sand;

the precise location of my father's grief,
& my mother's longing.

There is frost on my window
in the shape of an egret.

Outside the trees have begun
to button their white coats,
& apply their makeup.

I feel like an angel,

but it seems like everything
around me has already been blessed.

— Kareem Tayyar

Cake Face in Four Acts

after Anna Binkovitz

1: Cake Face as an act of discovery

I am thirteen at a boy's birthday party.
A boy that I like
and a birthday party I didn't want to go to
because I am thirteen and my body is at war with itself.
I can see some of the battlefields on my face.
An hour before the party starts my mother brings me into her bathroom,
pulls out the shiny silver compact that the woman at the Macy's counter
with green eyelids and bubble gum lips chose for her.
I sit on the counter with my back to the mirror while my mother
paints my face the way her friend taught her to in high school.
I turn to face the glass and see how the orange powder rests on my very pale skin
and for the first time in almost a decade
I am invincible.

2: Cake Face as an act of shame

I am invincible until I am thirteen at a boy's birthday party
wearing my mother's shade of makeup
and before we sing Happy Birthday, Julie
with her baby perfect vanilla sugar skin
pulls a candle from the box.
With fingernails like glass candy
she holds the candle to my eye level
almost touches my nose
and spits a new term at me
Cake Face.
And now while everyone else is singing I am choking.
I cry myself to sleep that night

but the next day when I look in the mirror
I ask for the makeup again.

3: Cake Face as an act of survival

I ask for the makeup again and again until I am fifteen and
my mother buys me my own.
All the pieces are from the drugstore and
none of them are the same color as my skin
but that doesn't matter, the goal is not to match
the goal is to cover
to erase
to pretend that Cake Face is enough armor to shield me
from the words in the hallways
and the girl in the mirror.
I pretend to think that they are laughing at Cake Face
not at me.
I pretend no one can see me.
I put pink blush on my cheeks
to pretend that I have to pretend to feel embarrassed.
I put black crayon under my eyes
because that means I can't cry until all the lights are off.
The boy says he likes girls with *natural beauty*
and I pretend I woke up like this.
I use Cake Face as crutch or really
as needle and life support until one day
another girl tells me she likes my eyes, the ones I made
and I love the way she paints her lips and soon
we can hold each other's hands behind our shields
and slowly, Cake Face becomes Artist.

4: Cake Face as an act of love

Now, when the man says my makeup does not look *natural*
I laugh.
I spent forty five minutes on myself this morning
shaping the woman in the mirror with my own hands

in my own likeness
with my own love
I will not let Mother Nature or God take credit for this.
Do you know what it feels like to love someone so much
that you wake up early every day to paint her like a sunset
because it makes her smile?
I do.

– Christina Brown

California Snow

At a literary slumber party
Gloria comes to me in dream,
as stunning as in the early days
of *Ms. Magazine*.
I've never had work, she says,
leaning close so I can see
the tautness of her skin.
You're still beautiful, I gush.
Your cheekbones! Such structure!
(even asleep, I'm a star-struck fan)
Nonsense, she says, *it's not my bones*
it's moisture. Of beauty,
this is all you need to know:
put nothing on your face
but California snow.

— *Donna Hilbert*

Chop Suey

after the painting by Edward Hopper

Light is always a major player
in a Hopper painting, and this one

is no exception. Two women—
friends, sisters? Sister-close at least—

huddle over tea by a restaurant window
while light leans in and listens.

Light chucks the chin of the bashful
sharer, strokes the shoulder

of her confidante and spills over
half the table. Light peers in through the window,

riffles the curtain, and pockets
the secret that may well prove

the downfall of these carefully-suited women.
They may be sharing what will break

one or both of them. But they have dressed
to present a solid front

with kohl-stroked eyes, coiffed hair
and rosebud lips. As well-staged actors

they await their cue to lift the teapot
and point the spout at the problem.

Like centuries of sisters before them
they square their chins, stiffen
their backs, and brace,
wearing light.

— *Terri Niccum*

Cinerama

the old Mack Sennett Studio
is still open for business.
I get in here from time to time
to work on car commercials
or music videos.
below the stages
there are three basement levels
jammed with artifacts
from comedy's golden age
some dating back to the studio's
grand opening in 1912.
old man Sennett, the slapstick king
built an empire
out of Keystone Cops,
and flying custard pies,
when film shorts were called flickers
and Echo Park
was called Edendale.

the first level below
is crowded with equipment.
we descend a short stairway
to pick through the rental lights and C-stands.
there is the sound of footsteps
and muted voices
from the busy stage overhead
the walls down here are painted red
and none of us ask why.

the stage managers tell stories
of late-night wraps, interrupted
by unexplained noises,
lights blinking on and off
or clamps and hand tools

falling from a wooden shelf
with a sharp crack.
they talk of voices and movement
just out of view,
and they speak of these occurrences
solemnly.

the second level below
is stacked with hundreds
of rolled canvas backdrops
that once served as
opulent ballrooms
or the shores of the Nile.
we wander down here on our breaks
hoping our walkies remain silent.
it is here that we are told
to be aware.
the cigar-chomping buffoon
in bowler hat, ill-fitting suit
and pancake make-up
may stumble past.
or we may catch a flash of
a sad-eyed waif
or an immaculate director in jodhpurs
lining up a shot
that will never be captured.

the third level, we are told,
is off limits.

the hours stretch into the night
and I move lights and route electricity,
directed by a voice from behind a camera.
we all stay quiet while another take unwinds.
in some places the old wooden floor
flexes under my weight,
the same boards

where Fatty Arbuckle, Harold Lloyd
and Charlie Chaplin once hit their marks.

outside
is the nine dollar glass of beer,
freeway traffic thick enough
to kill your soul
and the homeless,
grinding against each other
under the freeway overpass.
there is vomit on the sidewalks
of what once was called
Edendale.
I work into the night
hoping for something ethereal—
the smell of ancient tobacco,
laughter from the dark,
a faint echo of barrel-house piano.
I hope for magic tonight,
in the old Mack Sennett Studio.

— *Curtis Hayes*

Cold Shoulder

I can't tell you
what the quarrel was about.
We'd been married twelve years,
had kids, and busy with our lives.
That night we went to bed
mad at each other.
I turned and faced north,
he turned and faced south.
The next day he left
without saying good-bye.
At supper, he never said a word.
On the third day,
I still got the cold shoulder.
I was frantic, insecure
and wondered
Will we ever make up?
Everyone knew he was easy going,
but this side of him
I never expected.
I can't tell you how we made up.
This was the worst fight
of our married lives.
All I know is that in our case
silence was not golden.

— Barbara Eknoian

Countenance Connotated

facsimile of me
CALL FOR POEMS
Prompted, scripted, please include a bio

this page a stage
my words a costume
the poem, my makeup

planting words like seeds
throughout my paragraphs
arrogant flowers bloom

an attempt to connect
your unconscious with my
irrational ramblings

absurd ballads, visions unsung
trapped between the threshold
of those words, my summary

my visage reflected
a fictive deluge
on plain white, decorated

dreams of elephant god Ganesh,
thieves, writers, crows
and my hungry ego

white space/foundation
stanza/concealer
the poetic make up of being me

— Christopher Francis Hyer

Cover-up

I want makeup for my trauma.
Something to hide
the blemishes of my soul away,
a simple dab and brush
sparkling motes in the light
drifting like snow.

I want makeup that says
    I am okay
that tells others I am okay.
A red smile that doesn't seem pained
or covered dark circles from the pressure
of living in a cold,
can't-go-fast-enough world.

I want makeup as a mask
that I can wear when I want to feel
powerful or sexy or desired.
Applicators and the right shade of Normal
against the winterscape of daily life.

— K. Andrew Turner

Crossed

My mother is busily applying makeup
her veined hand steadying a compact
while in the other a foam rubber sponge
cleanses the years from her skin.

I can still see our faces in that mirror
like phases of the moon, as she arches
a wicked eyebrow—her way of saying, *I see you*—
mascaraed lashes haloing her eyes
dark hair hennaed a favorite eggplant-brown.

To touch it is to get on her bad side
and I don't want that, but place my hands there
anyway, on the pronounced swell of her skull,
burrow my nails in the long purple strands
iron at the roots. "You know I can't stand that,"
she threatens, menacing my reflection
with her own. She is Gemini, the Janus-faced.

Concealed deep in her genetic makeup
are annals of witchery. "Remember
that woman in my office, the one who made
my life a hell those many, many years?"

I try to recall which colleague, which office.

"She's in the hospital now. *Incurable.*"
This last word unfolds with lusty gusto
underscoring her message: *I did it. I put the hex on her.*

"This is what happens when people cross me
or—*godforbid*—my children." Now thirty years

after she'd cursed some nasty old bitch

out of her office job, I place my hands
on her hair again, what's left of it. "You of all people
should know I hate it when my hair is touched."

Who cursed her, I wonder, strapped her ghostly
bones to this wheelchair? Who did she cross

to merit this?
                        — Marc Alan Di Martino

A Curious Souvenir

There I was, trying to wrap my hands
around the space she left in me,
hoping to reshape it into something
new, something small—a piece
of paper folded six times left on a park bench.

When someone said, *At least you've
never been in love; it would
break you,* I didn't tell him my ribcage was
shuddering against my heart right then.
That I couldn't forget her hands, kept
remembering the curl of her after we had
exhausted words and skin, turned sleepy, felt known.

Finally I carved myself a space, but I only
found it in the absence of her. It
appeared in the doorway where
her body once stood.
I understand what "us" means
now that I don't say it anymore.

Some days, I think it was worth it—
loving her to lose her to find myself—
other days I remember how she looked
when she watched me, the heft
I could see in the asphalt of her eyes.

She used to pull
my hips into the
concave of her.
She made room for me
and I filled it
I made room for her
and she filled it.

I sit here trying to pick her
from my teeth, remembering the stories
we loved to make up together.
Our best one was always that love
was enough. We said it when our bodies
were lit matches: temporary, angry with lust.
We said it so often
I swear I believed it.

— Holly Pelesky

Dance

Union City, NJ

The summer after 8th grade
we plan to attend our first dance.
I'm filled with questions:
what to wear
and how to style my hair.
I go over to Debbie's house
for her to apply make-up.
I trust her judgment;
she's been to a modeling class.

As we approach St. Michael's,
I'm ready to change my mind.
I have to be pushed inside.
The kids stand in clusters
in the dimly-lit gym.
We nervously chat
in our small group of four.
Then a blue-eyed guy,
who could be a junior or senior,
asks me to dance.
We circle the floor slowly
to Nat King Cole's "A Blossom Fell."

When the dance is over,
I stand in the center of my friends
dazed by the music.
I've just stepped into my teen years
dressed in pink organza,
my hair upswept in a French twist.

— *Barbara Eknoian*

The Debt

> *What can't be made up must be burnt to the ground*
> — Unsigned graffiti at the former Fred C. Nelles Boys
>   Reformatory School, Whittier, CA, 2012

There's a knock at the door.
Your father, who does the answering,
opens it. A man you can't quite see
outside the door is saying something.

It's about your father, about his owing.
You can only see your father's tight face.
Your father shakes his head. No.
The door closes. The man leaves.

For the next few years the man keeps
returning. Each time his voice raises slightly.
Always your father must pay. Always there's a no.
Always the door closes. Always the man leaves.

Years later, after you've forgotten
all this, there's a knock. A small boy,
with a folded yellow note pinned to his shirt.
Your father takes it and reads it slowly.

He shakes his head. No.
The door closes. That's the end of that,
your father says. Or so you think and go about
the easy business of forgetting.

Years pass. The house gets older.
The paths are overgrown. It's been so long
no one can remember anyone
coming to the house or calling anymore.

So you're startled when there is a knock.

Firmer. Insistent. Not as before.
Your father doesn't come to the door.
You do the answering now.

It's a woman. Your age.
She says your house is on fire, your children are dead.
You shake your head. No.
You are mistaken. You close the door.

In a room a woman quietly sleeps.
Outside a ring of small children tumble and play.
You hear sirens. You smell smoke.
You shake your head *no no no*. You scream.

There's a knock at the door.

— Mark Olague

Erased by Nostalgia

My Uncle Mike told me to stop
looking in the rear view mirror
and hit the gas forward,
the only sensible way
to live free of my demons.
He drops me off on a
Long Beach street corner
at the end of the same day
I said goodbye
to my childhood home,
my last glimpse
through the window of
my dead mother's
bedroom where
her shadow
was last seen
past midnight
applying her
makeup behind
a bamboo shade
until she drowned
in her own
homemade
fountain of youth.
I found myself
in the cold ghetto
of my adulthood,
never to look
back again
at what made it
all full of such
mournful,
broken promise.

— Kevin Ridgeway

Eyelids

Shimmering makeup
reflects hot summer night quest—
trap, die, reapply.

— Nicole Martine Street

For Now

Death squints, as if he recognizes you
as someone whose youth he forgot
to be kind to, and hopes to make up
for it now, but only a little bit.

— Bill Mohr

Ford Flex

She said she could see
a small sliver of road gangster
peering out from underneath
my slacked collar
and buttoned sleeves.
I confirmed.
I was transforming,
and letting my insides out
one slice of swagger at a time,
flipping the faulty pigeons of my past
like quarters
and only accepting the coins
that land on tails.
Bald eagles.
Because I've been stuck
in heads,
my own and others,
for years.
And I no longer need the perception
of a dead president
to hold me back.
I've been walking on two legs
for too long,
missing out on action,
wallowing like a woodpecker
in a forest with no trees
while I could have been flying on four wheels
and flexible,
and free.
Ringing in the new year
with a fresh smile, wind in my hair,
and feathered wings that glide
for miles among the clouds

of beautiful
black
roads.

> *— Karie McNeley*

Gem-Ignited

How can I write a celebratory song
after a year like this, brother?
Disbelief in present grief. Shaking
the cold hand of my super soul boy
in a room of praises I don't follow.
Uniting one last time in the hollow
empty sinus gap where tears bellow:
a deafening symphonic horror tribute
that our twin green eyes see right through,
a brand new light gone prematurely mute!
I can try to dispute it but I didn't write
the heartbeat's constitution and
maybe by now my mind's notes
on life and delusions are moot.

**

My face making up your expressions.
I can't remember if they're mirrored
or if they're mine.
And I'm hopeful to be remembered but
scared to be mistaken for my better half
stuck forever beneath the surface of ground,
labeled with a polished stone,
Your name laid beneath the foot
of our family's founders.
Your body laid beneath the feat
of our family's survival.

— Karie McNeley

The Ghost of Stephanie

Stephanie had spooky eyes.
Sometimes when I looked at her
I saw a mouth stitched shut
with barbed wire.
One afternoon,
in Mrs. Tewinkle's third grade class,
I noticed Stephanie sitting in a puddle
of her own pee.
Her body trembling.
Her hands covering her face.
I watched as the liquid dripped from the chair
to the floor.
I raised my hand
just for a moment
then put it down.
A girl, caught wearing her mother's makeup that morning,
giggled and pointed at her.
Todd, who was in my catechism class,
pinched his nostrils together,
pretending to pass out.
Donna, the class clown,
told Stephanie she'd better wear Pampers to school
from now on.
Mrs. T's wrinkled face loomed over Stephanie.
Her shrill voice rose above the crescendoing laughter.
Stephanie, shivering, rose from her pee-filled chair
and silently made the walk of shame
to the nurses office,
tears falling down her face.

Sometimes when I'm in a room
filled with God's children,
their faces beaming with light,
I imagine the ghost of Stephanie

floating above their heads,
golden liquid falling on their hair
like a warm baptismal rain.
Their heads thrown back,
swallowing all the guilt and the shame.
The pee and the tears
cleansing them,
purifying them,
bringing her back home again.
Bringing Stephanie back to grace.

— Wendy Rainey

Grief is the thing with fur—

an angry Muppet clutching at your neck,
circling your head like a war bandage.

At museums you flee it room by room.
You try to make up with music and pancakes,
but piano irks it. It runs on nothing.

You begin to care about its feelings,
to anticipate its small rages.
It claws your ribs open to the air.
It climbs your spine; it thrives on a narrow ridge

of collarbone. You stop going to work.
And now everyone hopes you will kill it,
like that mother who finally
drives her children into the lake.

This is not that story.

— Oceana Callum

"hereditary"

I am the granddaughter of a seamstress
generationally hand-crafted with chiffon
and embroidered in silver beads

even if the fabric attracts a
cosmic static struggle
and the beads reflect my deflections

pointing and laughing
pointing and laughing
with that inherited oval index fingernail
sometimes with me sometimes at me

she doesn't deserve that look

mascara that clumps like a bird
stuck in an oil spill
or flakes onto my cheek
like the leftover ashes of a phoenix

a burning woman
burning burning
past the vacancy signs
of love motels and my old soul

and my own makeup
started with the cigarette burn scar
on my left arm that smolders
like a log trying to rekindle itself

I crumble into a pile of grey dust
spiders and raccoons and cats
creep out of the rubble

laughing and pointing
laughing and pointing
with their oval index fingernails

the dust scatters
I sparkle sparkle sparkle
they dance like a wind-up jewelry box
circles and circles around me

— *Cait Johnson*

I Am

The poem is overgrown with weeds, the poet the gardener
The poem is freshly dug earth, the poet the pallbearer
The poem prompts leaders, the poet challenges readers
The poem's wind exposes the poet's sun
The poem overwhelms the poet's need for analysis
The poem is the distance, the poet the runner
The poem is a consequence of a choice that the poet complains about
The poem is the straw that breaks the poet's back
The poem wants to get in your head, the poet wants your mind
The poem explains why the poet understands suicide
The poem is written between the lines, where the poet reads
The poem interrupts sleep, the poet reaches for pen and paper
The poem is peanut butter enjambment
The poet is the wry revision
The poem is a picture of the poet's first draft, once removed, twice revised
The poem needs flow, stated in form, the poet needs states of flow, formless
The poem is inadvertent adventure, the poet a blatant catastrophe
The poem defaces the Arc De Triomphe: "We have taken heads for less!", the poet wears a yellow vest
The poem is the god of thieves and writers, the poet overcomes obstacles
The poem is a satellite orbiting the poet
The poem travels 34000 miles per hour, the poet takes 42 years to get there
The poem is in constant communication with the poet
The poem is a mirror that has trapped the poet's reflection
The poem is the poet's makeup
The poem is, therefore the poet thinks
The poem is mine, I am the poet

– Christopher Francis Hyer

if the earth wore mascara

god is less ugly under a microscope
wears designer shoes
and swears like a trucker
en route to a leaky dive bar flooded with rain

god is saying this to you
eat red apples, and cherries
sing riffs to friends under the moon
on a desolate beach
all good lookin' and slick

god is uglier through a telescope
popping stars between fingers like pimples
throwing asteroids toward planets, using earth
as a personal game of risk!

god isn't here
they're away on business
in the Andromeda galaxy
specifically buying up the best views
for world war three on earth

god eats pickled eggs
in the Sierra Nevada mountains humming
hymns about Elon Musk and admiring
their creation of makeup

god is ugliest in person
coughs into hand, then extends
for a friendly introductory handshake
ready to spread disease and when refused
pukes on shoes while reciting a line from the tempest
tells you to "fuck off," hoping to make you cry

so they can watch some mascara run wet with tears
only to ask for a dollar claiming
"i can forgive all of your sins, for a buck"

— Zack Nelson-Lopiccolo

In Another Life

I was a maker of collages:

White lily & paperback,
polaroid & watch-band,
bow-tie & grass-blade,
driver's license & seashell,
silver dollar & makeup case.

If you had asked me then
what was the purpose
of my work

I would have said I hadn't
the faintest idea—

ask me now & I'll tell you
I was gathering up
everything I'd lost from
the life before that.

— Kareem Tayyar

Learning Make-up

My best friend's dad was in cosmetics;
she loaned me her make-up to put on
during the morning bus ride.
I was careful to save the eyeliner,
the mascara wand, for the longer stops.
Coming home at the end of the day
I rushed to the bathroom before Mother
could see my smudgy eyes and tarted
cheeks. Once before dinner, I slathered
green eye shadow, black mascara,
lots of blush and silver-white lipstick.
At the table, my father said, *What
happened to you?* and I burst
like a water balloon. *I just want to be
like everybody else!* My parents stared,
wordless. I couldn't stop sobbing.
Let her cry, he said. *This must have been
building for a long time*. In a few months
I would be 14, old enough for make-up.
But by then, I wanted to be a hippie,
leaving behind my newly-shaved legs,
nipple-hiding bra, and all those colorful
shiny tubes that used to dazzle me so.

— *Tamara Madison*

Life's Lovely Hit or Miss

Some tableaus require more oxygen.
A whiff of neon for thrill,
the streak of lipstick
for statement: Constant Coral
for acquiescence, Ruby Red
for pounce. Happiness?
A calliope of colors
in twisting tubes and
viola! An easy foliage
or plumage as the case may be,
the branding sting of lips.

If you prefer comfort over style,
there is no vein richer
than the fervent mammal
mother's milk, happy euphoria
leaking a warm gravity.
Everything that claims you
tags you. The babe's
beaded bracelet that echoes
the name we start out with—
and struggle all our lives
to live up to
or crawl out of—
right down to the morgue's
toe tag directing us
to that door out.

In life all is not equal.
Some shovels find treasure
at first thrust. Sometimes
it takes a continent's reach.
Sometimes it takes the deep ink
of tattoo to name us, others

just a stranger's hand
wrapping ours,
calling us found.

— *Terri Niccum*

Lorac Alter Ego: "Secret Agent"
(Or Other Uses for Lipstick Tubes)

A lipstick parade
twenty shades long

stands in formation
along the front
of my desk,
bullets exposed

like a firing squad.
I interrogate

each new tube, get it
to give up its secrets,

tease out a name.
This line, *Alter Ego*,

hits like a missile strike.
Shelled out, tubes transform:

it's a cyanide cylinder,
a way to pass contraband,

a vial of dimes—

I pick up the first hue,
a plum-brown number

with a silky finish
that hints at dried blood.

A trace of its shape
calls up smoky barrooms,

a woman in a floor-length skirt
with a thigh-high slit,
and décolletage
that plays peek-a-boo

with her navel. She's
a single-shot weapon,

a KGB operative
waiting for her handler,

a personal shopper
with a double life
furtive, the way I hide
from myself.

— Anne Yale

The Magician's Assistant

Sews herself back up every night, back stage, after
the show, after the spell's worn off, the makeup and
glitter, the stage lights dimmed, she sits at her mirror
bent over her own figure, needle pulling thread.

The operation as routine as square knots, she will
stand, rub blood out of wound, take a plug of
whisky, and a pull off something often unmentioned
smoke spiraling as she readies herself

To sharpen the saw, to clean and oil the toothed
edge—glistening prepares for tomorrow's show
where a new room full of strangers will gather
gasp-open mouthed

In suspense, half believing, half not, as the magician
cleaves her in two the applause is for his miracle
and not hers, though it is her body they watch, her body
they imagine long after the popcorn has gone stale.

— Kelsey Bryan-Zwick

Maidens, Made in the Shade

A go-go girl in the raw, fish out of water, a mere housewife
and stay-at-home mother just weeks ago, deracinated at
age 25 at Abner's 5, a go-go bar owned by the Mafia, I sat
upon a fat red satin cushioned stool in the red shag-carpeted,
red velvet wall-papered dressing room and gazed amazed
at my co-workers, the young, beautiful go-go girls named
Patti or Suzi Q or Linda Lee, Cher (not the real one), Jane
or Carol reflected in the bright floor-to-ceiling mirrors and
watched them put on makeup swiftly, expertly, smooth the
beige ooze onto their round cheeks, pert noses, Sophia Loren
jawlines and I awed as the girls gently glued tarantula-sized
false eyelashes onto their wide blue, green, hazel or brown eyes,
pooched out their lips to paint on pale pink lipstick, poofed up
their red, blonde, brown or black petal-curled hair piled high
on top of their perfect heads all the while telling their life
stories, how they got here to this noisy, dark, go-go bar and why:
the men who betrayed them, beat them, left them high and dry
(the way mine did, too), true stories so incredible, unbelievable but
you just can't make up stuff like that, the Truth always stranger than
fiction and finally tired of talking, they'd stand up, check to see
in the mirror if they still existed and then they'd inspect their smiles,
suck in their tummies, adjust their costumes, tug on their sparkly
sequined or frenzied-fringed bikinis, stuff into their bikini tops
their Baba au Rhum bosoms to reveal just-right ample cleavage
but just enough to impress and inspire the men, the maelstrom
of men, astronauts, doctors, lawyers, CEOS, salesmen, mailmen,
machinists, aerospace engineers who came in every day and waited,
waited outside the door for an hour to get into the place, then waited
for a table or a barstool to order beer, more beer, bottled, tap beer
to leer, cheer their favorite go-go girl, a maiden who'd been made
and re-made in the dark, noisy, shadowy-shade of men.

— Joan Jobe Smith

Make Believe

As a young boy, I loved make believe,
creating worlds in my mind that no one
else could see.

I lived to transcend the mundane
and fly with dragons,
wizards and fairies.
I dove into stories to escape
life as living was cruel
and in fantasy I conquered.

I would make up the stories
pulling from my favorite books
with characters like Gandalf
or Eilonwy by my side.

Still I make up stories
of far-fetched lands
with powerful magic
and skilled swordsmen
or flying battleships
and mystical ruins.
These stories still save me.

– K. Andrew Turner

Makeup

On a bad day,
she sits, holding
a glass of wine,
lips red.

Is that lipstick
or is that from the wine?
Oh women, I wonder—

the eyeliner, the red
lips, the pink blush
in that tiny face,
painted.

She covers
the truth of her lips,
powders up her high cheeks,
covers up the worry in her eyes

and her natural beauty.

Has she forgotten
the beauty from inside,
the beauty that money cannot buy,
beauty irreplaceable?

Oh women, I wonder.

— April Nguyen

Making the Bed

for Shannon Phillips

Makeup doesn't matter in the dark,
unless it's make-up sex,
but in daylight, maybe we make up
our minds a little slower,
then it's night again, a little faster,
make up a head fantasy,
her makeup running under her eyes,
it isn't sadness, more or less,
a giving and taking, making the bed
before the baby, making up for
lost time of what could have been
if only the past was made up of her
natural beauty in the morning afters,
making up a messy bed, making
a bed messy, our bed we sleep in
together, wake up to makeup
on the shoulders of my shirts,
yesterday's makeup on washcloths
hanging on the bathroom rack,
smiling reminders in mirrors,
in breakfast eyes, mascaraed eyes,
bedroom eyes, we make up the best
in each other, blush at our love,
the foundation of our faces.

– Brian Harman

Maquillage

> *"I can't decide if it's better to write less, but with spurts of greatness or more with poems I end up hating"*
> — Gary Soto

Notice the fence is wood
not wire. Yet, still charged
full of electricity. A devil
disguised as a dead tree.
The good men on either side
love and hate, lies and truth.
Lichen light electric across
the posts without a mumble
moving slower than snails. A slither
of something succumbed by stupidity.

Notice the fence is wire
not wood. Mute
and lifeless, stiff, cold.
The bad men all around,
lighting torches, setting wood
ablaze. Churning, and molten
Arsonist in pig's clothing.
Pork parading phallic
and ponderously foolish.

— *Zack Nelson-Lopiccolo*

Maybelline #148: "Summer Pink"

A gateway cosmetic,
the only thing I ever tried to steal.
In a drugstore two states away,
I sampled shades
on the back of my hand
before slipping *Summer Pink*
into the back pocket of my jeans
as casually as a gangster
with a hundred dollar bill.
I was thirteen.

I pictured my seventh-grade crush,
Kevin Crawford,
at the threshold, waiting,
just outside the door.
He would be the Clyde
to my Bonnie. On the lam,
we'd elope to Atlantic City,
unspoiled as the first
freshly scooped ice cream cones
of summer, forget all about
the nuns' prohibitions:
No lipstick, lest you rise up
like a fallen woman.
Hard enough
to hide a barely detectable shell pink
(let alone a budding sex life)
but I had to make my move. And I did.
And the woman behind the register
called me out.

Just seeing if it would fit in my pocket.
I always planned to pay for it.

And I did.

— Anne Yale

Not Your Average Absentee Landlord

Death is always
"swinging by,"
"just happened to
be in the neighborhood,"
as friendly as Mr.
Rogers' acquaintances.
"Need to make certain
that you're picking up
your mail. You didn't
respond to my survey
questionnaire about
recordings of bird
songs being too loud.
*Cheep cheep cheep
cheep cheep.* Nothing wrong
with a little D.C.
military band nostalgia,
eh? Common sense requires
me to test my front
and back door keys
at any hour I choose.
Sorry to wake you up
from your first nap
since the panel door
of the fuse box
gave you that twilight
vaporizing. Death
Reassurance Policies,
interested? Since when've
you been the beneficiary
you deserve to be? Any-
one can afford it. The first
half-century is free,
but I make up for

my generosity with a balloon
payment, two dollars
a year that I steal
from whatever tip jar
you have finally succumbed to
out of lackadaisical
compassion for those
who earn less
than you do." Death smiles,
and starts to note
how much work remains
to be done: termite
inspection, new
rugs, new stove,
a reconditioned
refrigerator, stain
remover. Yeah,
an extra bottle
of that for
the next tenant
to use after
moving in the day
after tomorrow,
though not
this year's tomorrow
of self-inflicted
sorrow.

— *Bill Mohr*

October

This evening I imagine you at a festival
off the coast of Big Sur,

your makeup somehow holding out
against the rain,

the starlight reading the T.S. Eliot poem
you have tattooed beneath your left breast.

There is music, of course,
one slow ballad after another

being sung by a woman
only a few years older than you—

She is dressed like a shaman
but knows nothing of the night.

It hardly matters.

You are as lovely as always,
especially when your body begins
to match the rhythm of the wind.

Were I there I would kneel before you,
& remain until you stopped dancing.

Which I would hope you would never do.

– Kareem Tayyar

Painting of a Female Joker

I helped you rearrange, declutter,
drag the desk out, move mirrors,
your mother's clock, your father's
Vietnam picture, your swap meet
painting of a female joker, hung
it in your apartment dining room
above the AC wall unit, the idea
of it being fun, fierce, badass,
Harley Quinn, Batman's titted
nemesis gripping a sharp, bloody
knife, her own self-image poker
card burning between two fingers,
hair a chemical green, grin
extended into makeup deliberately
toxic, as days and months passed,
every time I looked at it, where
we ate our oatmeal and eggs,
drank beers, played cards, games,
laid out puzzles too difficult
to finish, where we painted our
own canvases under the influence
of a late-night's drunken, smoky
nakedness, your serene, sandy
beach reflection, my amateur
interpretation of death, you taught
me to use complementary tones,
blues, reds, yellows, purples, we
tacked and balanced our paintings
on each side of the mirror over
the dining table, they seemed to hold
us together in our differences, but
more and more, whenever I'd come
by to pick you up or spend the night,
it was the painting of a female joker

that became the first face I'd see
when I entered the front door, you'd
be in the bathroom getting ready,
putting on your own makeup, I'd
sit on the couch and wait as it crept
in my mind, I'd wonder if it crossed
in yours, how you were adamant
about not taking it down, it felt like
her eyes and smeared smile became
yours, did you envision yourself
as her maybe without even realizing
it, I should have noticed that look
of mischievous foreshadowing,
that villainous approach to love.

— Brian Harman

Palette of You

copper taste of your lips
belies dread
smeared chaos in a kiss
reapplied glossy smile
restores calm

apply a new face
arrange yourself in the glass
layers of MAC and L'Oreal
a masterful mosaic of standards
forced on blushed cheeks

swaying crimson hips
command attention on the floor
you maintain a painted pout
but downcast eyes refuse to engage
with any prospective partner
your silhouette unyielding

cast-off clothes
sprawl across a bedroom floor
your shine dulls with the removal
of lashes and cat eyes
your naked face
closes in the light

— *Jay Michael Allyn*

Plastic Limbs

I am not a Barbie doll
with straight plastic limbs
perfect painted makeup lips
locked in a welcome smile

I am not so many things
a gymnast or a size four
not a girl who wears heels
or crosses her legs for you

What I am is a gift
my body is my vessel
it knows every secret I've held
every weight pushed against me

My body is a gift
my feet love me
and my legs are angels
wingless messengers of God

My hands tell my story
if you are listening close
they have the most to say
my hands are a voice

And the curve in my back
when I lie on my stomach
will hold precious treasure
for a pirate with the right map

— Sarah Thursday

The Plasticity of Existence

> *"Reality" resides not in the external*
> *form of things, but in their innermost essence.*
> — *Constantin Brâncuși*

On a thick table
in a kitchen in
Romania, thin
slices of bread lean
against each others' friction,

the heat of the oven still
inside, a story spilling
out of dark pockets.
Some truth forgotten
behind the surface. A hungry

boy, bullied, runs
away, returns to carve
a violin for the starving
silence, crude utensils—
utile, unitary, simple.

Doors. Tools. A make-
shift phonograph. Engagement
of space and continuous line
in grounding matter to find
some eternal truth.

A quest for the absolute.
A resolution to the major
seventh, the peasant labor
and the humble meal. The hunger
resolved. The weight under

it all essential: the base

as important as form in space—
the base note of a woman's
perfume like an ache in common,
caught in passing, cast

into permanence at last.
The pulse at the wrist captured
in time to reveal the hard
work of the heart. The being
within matter unseen.

The simpler essence still
to be discovered, still
until the flight of its spirit—
like the woman's best
laugh saved only for

the one who awakens her
pure joy. Behind
the door, another kind
of form released—steam
rising like a marbled dream

to extend the stack of dishes
in a stone sink, glistening.
A purity found immutable.
The implied ascent of scale
and light, and the busboy singing.

— *Grant Hier*

The poem about the straight girl who decided I needed a coming out intervention after she kissed me first

She painted her nails with whiteout
carving skulls, hearts by ballpoint
claimed she liked my apocalyptic poetry
and Sharpied epics down my leg.
Gutted men and pierced appendages
bled black through my blue jeans,
down our naked thighs.
She injected love letters in red-inked Bic
over my neck and shoulders
during duPratt's lecture on the gilded age
where pretty girls' affections destroy
only men.

– JL Martindale

Poem Without a Name

Some days love, I am built like a guillotine
nothing you say can save you. My mouth
gravity's weapon, blade's sharp chop. My glance
blank ouroboros stare. My eyes glassy
a one-way mirror staring contest, determined
to end this, because—my head rolls

The more I want our future together
the more I have to accept this truth—
that my bad days are becoming yours.
Days where it's hard to move, slow to walk
tight in my bones, achy tug-numb stuck
days where even your vise-grip foot rubs
won't make a dent in my rock-spasms

Days between diagnosis, pictured in black
and white digitized scans, photocopied
anxious bristled nerves. How to explain
to pour the doctor's words into your ears
without causing a flood? Without
drowning you, and all those that I love?

So, I stick out my elbows, point my teeth
thinking it might somehow be easier to twist
this love up into some other shape—call you
friend instead, cut you loose. I think about
how you could see other people, be happy

I would have time to read and write more
distract myself, sharpening my blade. Avoid
the issue, my own problems left unexplained
become less real, disappearing away from
everything. Reassured in my belief that nobody
could love a guillotine

But you see, it's the bad news I don't want
to share, and you don't waiver, or shake
or blink. Somehow you traverse all my pointed
and shiny broken mirror like edges, and you hold
you hold out, and hold on, and you hold onto me.
Sometimes neither of us says the right thing
but we make it up, we make up, we keep on
trying—we keep our mouths open.

— Kelsey Bryan-Zwick

Poem Without the Whole Truth About Sex

we never had great sex
we had not-exactly-an-affair sex
hurry-up-and-get-home-to-my-kids sex
we never had mind-blown sex
write-home-to-mother sex
we had stop-between-errands sex
forget-my-life-for-five-minutes sex
we had won't-look-you-in-the-eyes sex
don't-wrinkle-my-clothes sex
we never had first-waking-breath sex
never in-the-shower, -car, -kitchen, or -window sex
we had futon sex
we never had I'm-lucky-to-be-lying-next-to-you sex
never hot-make-up sex
we had let-me-call-you-"bad girl"-so-I-can-feel-less-bad
-about-just-needing-you-to-not-be-her sex
we never had I-love-you sex
never you-are-my-world sex
just had exploring-my-options sex
just if-I-keep-reminding-you-how-lost-I-am,
-you-won't-blame-me sex
never oh-my-fucking-god
can't-speak-after
where-did-that-come-from sex
just I-don't-know-who-I-am sex
just gotta-go sex
just sex

— Sarah Thursday

Portrait of a Sabine Woman

Oh! Her beautiful body, imagine
pecked at like angry swans
until she finds this stillness, framed
nothing moving except the faint
little trickles of blood; a sieve
her skin pours, the gleam of
frescos or oils in the right light.

It's this shade of red on my mouth
I remember as I put on my makeup.

— Kelsey Bryan-Zwick

A public house is being torn down

for Hillary 2016

She is grayer than I recall. Perhaps it's just this
November sky reflecting their disappointment,

perhaps it is just this light rain, or mist, playing
tricks on these old eyes?

But she looks grayer, none the less.

They have decided that they are going to tear her
down to make room for something that has no form,
or substance, a gilded, monstrous development to
house a bunch of vanities.

I came here tonight to say goodbye, to perhaps lean
against the old place, for one last time, and to pray
about the future.

I came here tonight, I suppose, to reminisce, and to
witness these passages wherein I had safely rambled
and dreamed, innocuous of the fierce elements
outside, storms that passed while I sat reading, or
playing all the while the elements beating against
the roof and windows... no concern of mine,

but now I understand how her lifetime of patches
and repairs are all being questioned

the honesty of the work scrutinized and those who
have never done an honest day's work in their lives
are now adorning themselves in a glory that was
never theirs to claim.

I saw a picture of what they want the
new development to be,

and as peculiar as it sounds, I swear that there were
the stars and bars of the old confederacy somehow
implied or projected on the buildings gaudy gold
façade

Maybe it was just these old eyes playing tricks on
me
but there *it* was, touching an old fear that percolates
up when symbols like that are seen.

I had contributed what I could, to save this old
place,

but it would have taken more than money to save
her.

We had expected that we had done enough, but
shenanigans perhaps it was always just a
swindler's hustle, but this felt different. Some say
the Russian oligarchs just took us over.

Some say it's always just a circus, and others say it
was the special interests that lost it for her, some
claim that the media paid into the crooked scheme
and that it was all of that free TV time that tilted
the playing field

so now the same old con men who seem to win
everything hoot and holler, they mock and taunt,
"We won, you didn't."

I don't care about the money but in pitching their
formless plan
they made this place sound so horrible, they

magnified her every flaw all the while hiding their
own imperfections they screamed about "progress"
and "draining the swamp" and oh they promised so

much and what hurts is that everyone knows that
it's not about what's true, it's about what you can
get people to believe.

So in the end the reality is, *this space*, may just lie
fallow, or even worse it may become a shallow
grave for what is true and we may wake up aimless

victims of an elaborate Ponzi scheme, like I said the
sad part is that everyone knows it's not about
what's true;

they rattled on about plush living with high walls to
keep out the undesirables

senior citizens restored to health, streets lined with
opportunity, and them whispering, "What have you
got to lose?"

In the end it appears that we've lost our dignity.

So I came by tonight to say good-bye and in this
quiet, gray November, I am amazed that the old
place never looked better.

Looking down I find a tattered, rain-soaked note
under my foot

When I pick it up it says,

"Let us not grow weary in doing good,
for in due season we shall reap,
if we do not lose heart."

In that moment it is as if all of the hope that she has ever had, has haloed her. It is as if all of the years of care have lit around her and in this quiet moment I wish that everyone had come and stood with her like this

so that they might really appreciated all that she had to offer.

— George Hammons

Reciprocate and Replicate

This failure-feigned heart
lies latent in your doorway.
Knuckles bruised from knocking
hard-headed oak for months.

No reply.

All these star-spangled attempts
to bring back a doomed-future fate;
a faded handwritten message
scrawled in tired, trembling black ink
shoved into an overstuffed mailbox.

No reply.

Remnants of history, gone soon
along with the walls and the roof,
but I'll hold close to toppled shambles
of discarded bookshelves I've turned into art.

No reply.

Gearing up for extremity's memories
to mark like scars, permanent derailment
of thought, trapped inside a thought,
and another. A riddle of heart and soul
memorialized on a shaken Etch A Sketch.

No reply.

And somehow hindsight still goes wild and strong
from this padded room with painted view.
An absence of frame makes it easy to reign,
reciprocate, and replicate so many visions of you.

— *Karie McNeley*

Red Chiffon

I hear the black crows calling
Brown mourning doves, blue scrub jays, iridescent hummingbirds
I'm no longer asleep, the birds are waiting
I don my green Michigan hat, walk outside
I see bees, lots of them, this is good: more bees, more pollination, more flora, mushrooms bloom,
happy days under grey skies
Peanuts for my friends, four handfuls, on the lawn, in view of my window
Now I sit and breathe
"Thoughts arrive like butterflies" is a song lyric, don't follow it, just breathe
I breathe in, I breathe out
27 minutes pass, because that's what time does
Time to write
I need to tell this student that his sex robot story is misogynistic at best, abhorrent at worst
"This story would be good if your audience were the type of young men who have a lot of experience with internet pornography"
Too harsh, go with "underdeveloped characters clip this story's wings" but mention how "aging" is not a reason for a woman to be the center of conflict, and that her "not being tight," and "getting laid" are not compelling reasons to read a story
I use the word "problematic" instead of "sophomoric"
I write about others, their work, their words
I will not shower today, I refuse to believe that lack of self-care is a symptom of depression
I haven't had a drink in two thousand and four days, I feel nothing about this
I walk past my therapist's office, unofficially cancelling my appointment
I am breaking up with him
I did not like the way he wrote when I confessed that I feel nothing
I did not like the way his eyes smiled when I told him about the

    time I put on a dress and applied
makeup
I am breaking up with him
I think it's Wednesday. I know it doesn't matter.

— Christopher Francis Hyer

Revlon #415: "Pink in the Afternoon"
(Audrey Hepburn's Favorite Shade)

Pink in the Afternoon puts a little life
back into the faces of the dead.
It's the mortician's beauty secret.
Embalming can make the dearly departed
look like they've lost their lips.
And you can't exactly use
a lip-plumping product, you know?
It has no effect on a corpse.
Besides, the esthetician's goal
is to make your loved one
look as natural as possible—
at peace, even—
not to wipe out all the imperfections
earned by living. Take too much away
and you get in trouble with the family.
Add just a hint of color,
and they still look like themselves,
about to wake,
just in time for *Breakfast at Tiffany's*.

— Anne Yale

Revlon Super Lustrous Lipstick, Crème Color #640, Blackberry: Part I

> *The curve of your lips rewrites history.*
> — Oscar Wilde

We cruise the aisles
of Skaggs Drugstore, fingers
trailing the glossy covers of *Vogue,*
Seventeen, Ms. We practice
sloe-eyed glances, pout
at our own reflections.

Every tube is labeled *Try me*.
Streaks of pink and coral
ladder our forearms. We kiss
the backs of our hands, seek
the miracle to ripen us.

Every lipstick is
too pale, ghosts
of kisses never landed,
no shade strong enough
to compete with cinnamon skin.

From the last black lacquer tube
color #640 emerges
Disney-villain dark—
poison apple, magic potion
sand running through a witch's hourglass.

It looks black one friend says,
Like blood. The other friend shrugs,
turns back to the rows of Barbie hues.

I lean toward my reflection
and swipe Revlon across my lips,

hopeful. My sixteen-year-old self falls
away; in her place, a woman
who blooms cherries, breathes garnets.

— *Aruni Wijesinghe*

Revlon Super Lustrous Lipstick, Crème Color #640, Blackberry: Part II

> *With my mask, I controlled all of the mouth movements with my own mouth.*
> *— Peter Mayhew*

his thumb wipes the stain
from my lips

You know what they say,
he growls.
The darker the berry,
the sweeter the juice.

looks at the smudge
on his fingerprint,
rubs the dark
on the thigh of his jeans

my naked mouth
defenseless

— Aruni Wijesinghe

Saying Things With Our Hands

I think we machinists have done pretty well
at our machines
making things
too many politicians have strutted
the world stage as the cameras clicked and the lying words poured
    from their mouths
and the people suffered
and died
too many wars have raged
over empty words shouted out of the mouths of emperors with egos
    the size
of empires
we stand
in front of our machines turning blocks of raw steel or aluminum
    or titanium
into bridges
wheelchairs
scalpels for surgeons
axes for firemen axles for ambulances valve blocks
for oxygen masks so people in crashing airplanes can survive too many
Mussolinis on balconies Capones with their fingers on machine
    gun triggers have opened
their mouths and ordered us around so they could feel
big
we carve brass into trumpets blowing notes
bright enough to save lives under midnight stars
make stainless steel keys
unlocking libraries full of Shakespeare plays
trains could not roll telescopes could not focus buildings
could not stand without us and as our machine cutters
make piles of sharp shiny steel or magnesium chips
we look down at our hands
and smile
we do not need words

does the nightingale singing its heart out under the full moon need words
did Charlie Chaplin
twirling his cane down the open road though he didn't have a
    penny in his pocket
the Mississippi River
taking Mark Twain through the fog as he gripped the steamship wheel
what words
could explain Van Gogh's swirling stars the panther's orange eyes
    burning
in the jungle night
or teach Nureyev
how to hang in the air as if he would never come down
and we look down at our hands
and smile
let the presidents and kings pound their chests and shout
we stand solid and true
as the Golden Gate Bridge shining
in the dawn sun.

                    — Fred Voss

She Died of Her Own Beauty

She was putting on her face
when her mind exploded
behind its pretty facade
and left the lipstick
bloody against her lips,
her broken teeth
all smiling in
gruesome defeat,
a fallen Avon customer
who got turned to dust,
but her beauty is
immortal in the faces
of her sons after
she was whisked away
to a place where there's
no space or time for her
to battle the war
on her perceived
ugliness again,
laughing at us when we
couldn't figure out
what to do with
the mountain
of cosmetics
she left behind.
They painted a mask
she hid behind when
she confronted
the ugliness of the world.
A single parent renegade
who stared beyond
the miniature spotlights
that surrounded her
vanity mirror,

where she painted
one final, tragic beauty
across her lifeless face.

— Kevin Ridgeway

Supernatural Phantom Woman

She never wore makeup,
never needed it in her plain beauty.
It's a terrible thing to hide underneath
the war paint she washed off
during the women's movements
of her progressive youth,
when she danced on barroom tables
and wrote poems that sang
the gut-wrenching beauty
inside of her, bringing her to tears
whenever she would attempt
to read her own poems,
and so I read them aloud
with her in a motel bathtub
shaving her legs until her
separation from the pen
made her fall onto
the cutting room floor,
where voices are
no longer heard.

— Kevin Ridgeway

Test

My first psychological test
was a *Dell Pocket Quiz*
found in my father's bathroom drawer.
It was full of questions like
Do you love one parent more than the other?
Did you ever wish one parent were dead?
Do you ever think of suicide?
To all of this he answered *yes*.
I asked my mother about the quiz.
She said for me not to worry
that the quiz belonged to someone at his work.
As far as I know, that was the only intentional lie
she ever told me.

— *Donna Hilbert*

The Thing About Love and Flowers

The dining room table tulip petals were reaching,
splitting open like sunset-lidded salsa skirts,
as I studied the effortless heart of blooming,
I asked,
If you could give one piece of advice,
what would you say makes a lasting relationship?

And I watched her blurry blue eyes look up and to the left
watched her sort through sixty-seven years of scribbled grocery lists,
of her son Leo's dinosaur phase when she stepped on a
forgotten pterodactyl figurine in the middle of the night
and broke her arm and the rocking chair her grandmother had
    given her,
the time Hugh emerged from the wrong side of the hallway,
when they were staying in that hotel with that unsavory woman,
his voice that night, littered with scotch and resentment,
the answers that never quite made sense

the farm house in Maine where they made love on the creaky table,
before the Parkinson's that hijacked her motor skills,
before the Alzheimer's that turned his Harvard brain into
    waterfalls of rambles,
that rainy St Patrick's day, pants half off, hair alive with rainwater
lips plump with bourbon, ass sticking to the wood table,
whispering I-love-yous,
trying not to wake her sister and brother-in-law in the next room.

Space,
she finally replies,
giving someone their space is important,
and I agree and say that he didn't honor my space,
that I was one of his drugs of choice, a dangerous collusion that
    cost too much,
and I go on to say that I believe that when we let go of what's dead,

we can offer more energy to our roots,
that I believe that I will find something healthier,
and she says
maybe.

She clears her throat,
traces the wood pattern on the table with a shaky finger, and says,
there were a few who I thought might be a better fit,
but I was where I was.
It was 1947.

And I knew that my question was empty,
I know well enough that there is no secret,
that some loves are crumbling maps to the detonator
that some eyes disrobe our guards
as they embed a story deeper than time,
and that some loves sit safely atop the skin,
like a mosquito net in the middle of the Amazon
or a charming piece of costume jewelry that slowly turns the finger
    green.

I look back to the tulips
faces aching with the weight of beauty
and wonder how much longer until the song of skirts will become
limp, wrinkled melodies, scratched records that once turned and
    burned,
remember that answers are
justifications for shades of regret.

I will wear the questions like sacred spring buds,
will dance like fire is holding my serpent spine hostage,
I will inscribe my hips with the prayers of lovers,
I will hold hearts like baby birds and I will
place mine on the tongue of uncertainty

I will be terrified, dangerous, broken,
a vial of luminous grief in fluid woman form,

I will be brave in my vase of skin,
I will look back and say,
yes, that sojourn,
that misstep,
that glorious fall
it was in the reaching that I bruised
it was in the reaching that I bloomed.

— Melissa Lussier

This poem is made up

for the man
whose mother wanted a girl.
This poem is rage. Cage.
Dress up.
This poem is bad intentions.
This poem cannot be made right.
Like some makeover.
Or the man in the dress.
This poem is for the woman
who loved him anyway.
This poem refuses to lie.
This is how he makes her up.
Because mother.
Because dead ringer.
Is this how you like it?
he asks them both
but not at the same time.
This poem is down low,
is the man's made-up life.
How he's barely in it.
This poem refuses to loft.
This poem is for the man
and his mother.
How they pass it down.
Mother to son.
Husband to victim.
How they escape.
But don't.
Because you can't
make these things up.

— Alexis Rhone Fancher

Trace

I've given up
underwear, shoes.
I wash my face
but wear no make-up.
My jewelry waits
in a box at home.
My hands are tan now,
betray no trace
of my life before.

— *Donna Hilbert*

Trigger

Sometimes a trigger is like a gun. Like a crack, a bang, a shook awake. Sometimes a trigger is like a flinch, a twitch, a tendon snapped. A trigger over and over all day looks like a hunched back, like stomach hurts, like tired after a long night's sleep, like if I work too hard all the time it's easier to explain the dark circles covered with makeup. Sometimes a trigger is like a bomb, a mushroom cloud blooming black sky, like a loud you have to cover your ears. Sometimes a trigger is like a gone quiet, like dead eyes, like a tranced face. A trigger scraped across dead skin looks like a map, like an ocean in drought, like a flickered light.

— Sarah Thursday

Truth

My husband has predicted the imminent fall of three trees: a spruce discovered after cutting to have rotted hollow; a dogwood that would have landed on his car had he not felt a threat and moved it; and a Douglas fir that he warned a neighbor about, but she rebuked him: "It's my tree, don't touch it." After which it fell on her house.

Given his reputation, brother Robert and partner Mixel ask him to assess the danger of surrounding redwoods five times the height of their mid-century Seattle home. Glimmers of sunlight peak through, patio dappled, koi nurtured in shade.

He laughs, but looks hard. Does he feel disaster looming, a fish bone innocent until the throat is pierced.

Removal requires a permit. Trees are given the status of cows in India, revered wholly, and therefore, allowed to squeeze the driveway into a thin wavy line as trunks add rings. Our fingers cross.

I look up often, not in fear but in awe. Pine air and birdsong lure me. My steps skirt moss, press into loam. I reach out my hands to touch the rough bark, feel a pulse.

Up the hill, an elderly neighbor heard a boom as night fell, and watched as neighbors cut cedar and hauled huge hunks of another near miss. Mixel asks again—is this one leaning toward the bedroom? Not one to make up a story, my husband simply says he isn't sure.

Old trees say nothing,
yet truth is found among them.
Find yourself here. Breathe.

— Nicole Martine Street

Unforgettable

I am always trying to become unforgettable
always trying to become the kind of girl
who can walk on the beach without kicking sand up behind her
the kind of girl who doesn't count calories
but still fits into all her best friend's clothes.

I want to be the kind of girl who leaves
a handprint, a polaroid,
a small tube of moisturizer in every ex lover's apartment
a makeup stain on your favorite t-shirt
just specific enough to remind you of me.
When I say I am always trying to become unforgettable
I mean that if I am only remembered in small, pretty pieces
then I want to be the one to choose them.

I don't mean I don't want you to move on.
It's just that when the new girl suggests
you go to her favorite museum for your second date
I want it to always be my favorite museum first.
I want you to remember me there in a sundress
how I walked beside you from exhibit to exhibit all afternoon
and didn't shiver from the air conditioning
not even once.

And I don't want to be better than her.
When I say I am always trying to become unforgettable
I mean I am always trying to become irreplaceable
and so, I pretend that my secrets are more interesting than they are
I pretend that my body knows and wants more than is the truth
I pretend to think that everything is fake unless I say it isn't.

I will myself permanent, believing that maybe
if I learn to slice an avocado into perfect little moons
if I time the bread in the oven and the meatballs on the stove just so

and serve every dish hot and at the same time
maybe then mine will be the kind of voice that echoes
maybe then I'll be pretty enough to be called haunting.

And it's not that I really want to haunt you
it's just that I want to last the way you will.
I know I will hold you somewhere in me
long after we've stopped loving each other.
I can cleanse all of my rose quartz with selenite and sage and still
I will have held them when I loved you.
I can move once, twice, three times and still
some of my things will always have been mine when I loved you.
I can put all of the ticket stubs and presents
in a shoebox and hide it in the back of my closet and still
I will have loved you.
I will fall into a good, new love and still
I will have loved you
and I want this whole and uncomplicated truth
to be the story you remember.

When I say I am always trying to become unforgettable I mean
I don't love you anymore
but I want it to matter that I did once
that I tried
and that now I am somewhere else
and I am not in love with you
and maybe,
if I can't control which parts of me you display and discard
I think I would rather be forgotten after all.

— Christina Brown

The Warehouse

Like air from a bellows
your breath rises.
You sleep in the deep
underwater of dreams.

My mind scratches
at the skin of things,
takes me down the road
to the warehouse.
I know the way, it's my
favorite place to visit.

My old files
are stored here
stacked high in
ratty cardboard boxes.
Inside, the lights
burn hot and bright
so the small print
is easy to read.

Forklifts rattle inventory
to the loading dock.
My stupid heartbreaks
are ready to ship.

I feel your breath
on the back of my neck.
You swim closer
to me in your dreams.
I shut off the lights,
dive into your sea.

— Tere Sievers

Will You Ever Stop Wanting Me?

His eyes keep saying
blinking, always waiting
for me to take him again,
he loves to feel my lips
open wide above him,
his mouth wider ready
to swim in the savor
of my stickiest sensations.
He loves to explore
with tongues savoring
journeys inside my softest
of gardens revealing my most
thorniest of flowers,
wickedly tempting him,
my mister always forgets
about the ring on his finger,
I distract him with my gushing
temptation, I grind above his
starving face, so clear, he worships
my every taste, never stop
sprinkling, before making me
erupt, I always love checking
my look on his naked reflection,
he is like my favorite
make-up mirror,
always imagines us closer
than our bodies appear.

— *Adrian Ernesto Cepeda*

Wrong Number
(The only question worth asking)

Trying to plan my week,
I drew a grid on the page
to slip over the future,
fill in the numbers,
and address the days
one at a
time.

But counting
by days of the week
the spaces between,
I discovered
an extra line drawn,
and so, one too many
days.

I decided to keep it in.
After all, it was due
to arrive tomorrow,
so I might as well wait
and live through it
at least once before
scratching it out of existence.

That being decided, I was faced
next with the question
of what I should do with it.
What could I do?
Save a life?
Buy beans and beer?
Bread and wine?

Or sleep through it,

exhausted from
the previous seven,
then awaken
and begin anew,
maybe even
another eight days?

Let the others remain limited
in their Gregorian litany,
I was growing to like the idea
of this newfound time, whatever
it was called—not having labeled
like all the other days, no need
to invent a new name now.

The next morning
I was awakened by
my own voice: I had
not heard the phone ringing,
but my pre-recorded
greeting answered
for me.

After the beep,
a person I didn't recognize
began talking about someone
else I didn't know. Being
that this was the first new
day, I thought they might
know something I didn't.

I decided to not pick up,
but to listen carefully
and take their advice
without question, flooded
with relief just to think
that a stranger could know

better about my life than I.

I'd been wrong too many times,
it was clear. The voice told me
I should forget about yesterday's
mistake, to call that other person
I didn't know and to let them know.
I unplugged the clock
and dialed my birthday.

— *Grant Hier*

Recommended Reading

"Cover-up" p. 20 w/ "Trigger" p. 91

"Dance" p. 25 w/ "Maybelline #148: "Summer Pink" p. 54

"Makeup" p. 50 w/ "Supernatural Phantom Woman" p. 84 & "Trace" p. 90

"Red Chiffon" p. 74 w/ "This poem is made up" p. 89

Acknowledgements

"Ashtray" and "Beans" first appeared in *Gravity: New & Selected Poems* (Tebot Bach, 2018).

"Because the sky was soft and slow" was originally published in *Similitude* (Pelekinesis, 2018).

"Cake Face" was first published in *Fight Evil With Poetry* (Sideshow Media Group, 2018).

"Dance" was first published in *Why I Miss New Jersey* (2018).

"Ford Flex" and "Reciprocate and Replicate" were first published in *Redshift*.

"The poem about a straight girl who decided I needed a coming out intervention after she kissed me first" first appeared in *Like a Girl: Perspectives on Feminine Identity* (Lucid Moose Lit, 2015).

"Painting of a Female Joker" first appeared in *Suddenly, All Hell Broke Loose!!!* (Picture Show Press, 2020).

"Poem Without the Whole Truth About Sex" was first included in *Conversations with Gravel* (Sadie Girl Press, 2018).

"Test" first appeared in *Deep Red* (Event Horizon Press, 1993).

"Trace" first appeared in *Transforming Matter* (Pearl Editions, 1999).

"Wrong Number (The Only Question Worth Asking)" was originally published in *The Difference Between* (Pelekinesis, 2018).

Adrian Ernesto Cepeda is the author of *Flashes & Verses... Becoming Attractions* from Unsolicited Press, *Between the Spine* published with Picture Show Press and *La Belle Ajar*, inspired by Sylvia Plath's 1963 novel, will be published by CLASH Books in 2020.

Alexis Rhone Fancher is published in *Best American Poetry, Rattle, Hobart, Verse Daily, Plume, Tinderbox, Cleaver, Diode, Poetry East, Pirene's Fountain, Flock, Duende, Nashville Review,* and elsewhere. She's authored five poetry collections, most recently, *Junkie Wife* (Moon Tide Press, 2018), and *The Dead Kid Poems* (KYSO Flash Press, 2019). Her photographs are featured worldwide. A multiple Pushcart Prize and Best of the Net nominee, Alexis is poetry editor of *Cultural Weekly*.

Anne Yale is a poet, educator, and editor. She is also the author of *Liturgy of Small Feathers* and *What's That Word?*

April Nguyen is a student at California State University, Long Beach.

Aruni Wijesinghe is a project manager, ESL teacher, sous chef and belly dance instructor. She is an emerging voice and has been published by *Angels Flight—Literary West*, Moon Tide Press, Picture Show Press, Arroyo Seco Press, *Altadena Poetry Review* and others. She lives a quiet life with Jeff, Jack and Josie.

Barbara Eknoian is a poet and novelist. She is a long-time member of Donna Hilbert's poetry workshop in Long Beach where she's happy to practice her craft. Her poetry books and novels are available at Amazon. She lives in La Mirada, CA with son, daughter, three grandsons, and three dogs (which she never picked out). She's never lost her Jersey accent.

Betsy Mars is a prize-winning poet, photographer, and educator, who recently took up publishing as well, releasing her first anthology, *Unsheathed: 24 Contemporary Poets Take Up the Knife* (Kingly Street Press, 2019). She was educated at the University of Southern California, and occasionally puts what she learned to use. Her work has been published in *The California Quarterly*, *The Ekphrastic Review*, *Rattle* (photography), and numerous other online journals and print anthologies. Her first chapbook, *Alinea*, was published by Picture Show Press.

Bill Mohr is a professor of literature and creative writing at California State University, Long Beach. His most recent collection of poetry is *The Headwaters of Nirvana* (What Books, 2018). His blog can be found at billmohrpoet.com. Website: koankinship.com.

Brian Harman was born and raised in Orange County, CA, where he can be found trying new craft beers, creating themed playlists, and rooting for the Angels. His work has been published in *Chiron Review*, *Nerve Cowboy*, *Misfit Magazine*, and elsewhere. His poetry mentors include Gerald Locklin and Charles Harper Webb.

Cait Johnson is an undergraduate at Long Beach State. Her poems have been featured in *Left Coast Review* and *Alchemy Literary Press*.

Christina Brown is a writer and educator living in Orange County, CA. Her poems, short stories, and essays have been published in places like *Fight Evil With Poetry*, *Broken Pencil Magazine*, *SKEW*, and *The American Papers*.

Christopher Francis Hyer: "Look how arrogant I am, I put my name at the top of the page! This is my bio of 50 words that should be included with my submission. I am called Chris. I am a student of Creative Writing at CSULB, but you already knew that. I am having the time of my life reading and writing and I am over the word count."

Curtis Hayes has worked as a grip, gaffer, and set builder in film production. He's been a truck driver, a boat rigger, a print journalist and a screenwriter. A Southern California native, he is a graduate of the California State University, Long Beach, Creative Writing Program and his poetry has been featured in *Chiron Review*, *Trailer Park Quarterly*, *Cultural Weekly* and other small presses.

Donna Hilbert's latest book is *Gravity: New and Selected Poems* (Tebot Bach, 2018). Her work is widely anthologized, most recently in *Is It Hot In Here Or Is It Just Me?: Women Over Forty Writing On Aging* (2019). She has led workshops for both beginners and professional writers in venues as varied as a men's prison, an English public school, and literary programs including Aldeburgh Poetry and Ilkley Literature Festivals in the UK, and PEN Center USA West's Emerging Voices Rosenthal Fellows. She writes and leads private workshops in Long Beach, C, where she makes her home.

Fred Voss has had three collections of poetry published by Bloodaxe Books (UK), the latest of which, *Hammers and Hearts of the Gods*, was selected as Book of the Year 2009 by The Morning Star (UK) and was reprinted by Pearl Editions (Long Beach, CA). It is available on Amazon, along with his first novel, *Making America Strong*.

George Hammons is a Southern California poet whose work has appeared in *American Mustard III*, *Cadence Collective*, and *The Pacific Review*. He was featured in the photo and poetry blog, *Portraits of Poetry* (March, 2018). George studied creative writing, with a focus on poetry, at California State University, San Bernardino. He is the author of the chapbook, *Hungry to Bed*, from Arroyo Seco Press.

Grant Hier is a professor of English and creative writing at Laguna College of Art and Design. He is also the poet laureate of Anaheim.

Holly Pelesky is a lover of spreadsheets, giant sandwiches, and handwritten letters. Her essays have appeared in *The Nasiona* and *Jellyfish Review*, among other places. Her poems are bound in *Quiver: A Sexploration*. She holds an MFA from the University of Nebraska. She cobbles together gigs to pay off loans and eke by, refusing to give up this writing life. She lives in Omaha with her two sons.

Jay Michael Allyn is a composer, songwriter and emerging poet. He has tended bar at LAX, Rolling Stone Bar and Grill, The Proud Bird and has taught bartending classes in the L.A. area. He lives an introspective life in South Central where he continues to pursue music and writing.

JL Martindale spent the first half of her life in the valley (like for sure, for sure), but returned to her city of birth to attend California State University, Long Beach, where she earned a BA in English with an emphasis in Creative Writing.

Joan Jobe Smith was a go-go girl for seven years (1965-1972) before going back to college for the knowledge, getting Golden West AA, CSULB BA & one-year of law school & UCI MFA, founding *Pearl* magazine and *Bukowski Review*; award-winning Joan Jobe Smith, a Pushcart honoree has had her art, poetry, reviews, fiction, essays, poet interviews, recipes published internationally in more than 1000 places + 27 books/chapbooks, most recently, her prose memoir, *Tales of an Ancient Go-Go Girl*, and her new & selected poetry collection from NYQ: *Moonglow Á Go-Go*.

K. Andrew Turner writes queer, literary, and speculative prose and poetry. In 2013, he founded *East Jasmine Review*—an electronic literary journal. His full-length poetry collection *Heart, Mind, Blood, Skin* is now available from Finishing Line Press. He was a semifinalist for the 2016 Luminaire Award.

Kareem Tayyar's novel, *The Prince of Orange County*, is available from Pelekinesis Books, and his new collection of poetry, *Immigrant Songs*, was published by WordTech (2019). A recipient of a 2019 Wurlitzer Fellowship for Poetry, he holds a PhD in American and Poetry Literature from U.C. Riverside.

Karie McNeley is a poet, artist, and student from Lakewood, CA. Her poetry has been published in *Verdad!*, *Pagan Friends*, *Tears In The Fence*, and elsewhere. She is the founding editor and lead artist for Toucan Salsa Press.

A 2019 Best of the Net nominee, **Kelsey Bryan-Zwick** is a Spanish/English speaking poet from Long Beach, CA. The author of *Watermarked* (Sadie Girl Press), Kelsey's poems appear in *petrichor*, *Cholla Needles*, *Rise Up Review*, and *Redshift*. Currently, she is writing towards her new title, *Here Go the Knives*.

Kevin Ridgeway is the author of *Too Young to Know* (Stubborn Mule Press). Recent work has appeared in *Slipstream, Chiron Review, Nerve Cowboy, San Pedro River Review, Main Street Rag, The Gasconade Review, Trailer Park Quarterly, Misfit Magazine, Plainsongs, The Cape Rock* and *The American Journal of Poetry*, among others. He lives and writes in Long Beach, CA.

Marc Alan Di Martino is a Pushcart-nominated poet and author of the collection, *Unburial* (Kelsay Books, 2019). His work appears in *Rattle, Baltimore Review, Palette Poetry, Rivet Journal* and many other places, including the anthologies *Unsheathed: 24 Contemporary Poets Take Up the Knife* (Kingly Street Press, 2019) and *What Remains: The Many Ways We Say Goodbye* (Gelles-Cole, 2019). He currently lives in Perugia, Italy with his family.

Mark Olague is an Assistant Professor of English at Cerritos College in Norwalk, CA. He currently lives in the Lakewood Village neighborhood of Long Beach, CA.

Melissa Lussier, a self-described bird of paradise, originally hails from Buffalo, NY, and has enjoyed dancing with LA for the past four years. In addition to being a singer/songstress, she is a poetess, aesthetic creatress, proud feminist, and teacher of English. She loves ducks, salsa dancing, and adventures with no destination, and she believes in the redemptive power of deep vulnerability and hope.

Nicole Martine Street teaches English for the University of Hawaii; founded California State University, Long Beach's HipPoetics; hosts poetry readings at Kaua'i Community College; and also teaches yoga; gardens; paints; hikes; swims. Married in 2017 to Erik Horsley.

Born in the Costa Rican jungle, **Oceana Callum** grew up in the tamer orchards of Winters, CA. She holds an MFA in creative writing from CSULB, and her most recent poetry publication is in *Cider Press Review*. She lives in San Clemente, where three wild boys inhabit her house.

Sarah Thursday, in addition to writing poetry, co-hosted 2nd Mondays Poetry Party, ran a poetry website called CadenceCollective.net, and founded Sadie Girl Press as a way to help publish local and emerging poets and artists. She has been published in many fine journals and anthologies, interviewed by Poetry LA, and received a 2017 Best of the Net nomination for "To the Men who told me my Love was not enough." Her poetry books are available at SadieGirlPress.com. Find and follow her to learn more on SarahThursday.com, Facebook, Twitter, or Instagram.

Suzanne Allen teaches writing. She is a Pushcart Prize nominee with poems published in journals and anthologies around the world, such as *Cider Press Review*, *Pearl*, *Nerve Cowboy*, *Not a Muse: the Inner Lives of Women* (Haven Books); *Veils, Halos & Shackles* (Kasva Press); and *Villanelles* (Everyman's Library Pocket Poet Series). She is a co-editor of *The Bastille: The Literary Magazine of Spoken Word Paris*, and the founder of Small Fish Big Pond. Her first chapbook, *verisimilitude*, is available from Corrupt Press. She lives in Long Beach with her Shih Tzu, Filou.

Tamara Madison is the author of the chapbook, *The Belly Remembers*, and two full-length volumes of poetry, *Wild Domestic*, and *Moraine*, all published by Pearl Editions. Her work has appeared in *Chiron Review, Your Daily Poem, A Year of Being Here, Nerve Cowboy, The Writer's Almanac*, and other publications.

Tere Sievers lives and writes in Long Beach, CA and teaches at the Osher Lifelong Learning Institute at CSULB. She has been published in *Pearl, Verve, Staple, Genre, A Year of Being Here*, Silver Birch Press, and *Nerve Cowboy*. Her chapbook, *Striking Distance*, is available from Arroyo Seco Press.

Terri Niccum's newest chapbook, *Dead Letter Box*, was issued in October 2019 by Moon Tide Press. An earlier chapbook, *Looking Snow in the Eye*, was published by Finishing Line Press. Her work has recently appeared in *Nimrod International Journal, Lummox Poetry Anthology 8, The Maine Review*, and *Oberon Poetry*, among others.

Wendy Rainey's first book, *Hollywood Church: Short Stories and Poems*, was published by Vainglory Press. She is a contributing poetry editor on *Chiron Review*. Her poetry and short stories have been featured in *Nerve Cowboy, Trailer Park Quarterly, Red Fez, Hobo Camp Review*, and *Chiron Review*, among others. She studied poetry with Jack Grapes in Los Angeles and creative writing with Gerald Locklin at California State University, Long Beach.

Zack Nelson-Lopiccolo is a surfer, writer, editor, drywall taper, and constantly evolving being of the planet earth. From time to time poems are published, waves are caught, cats are snuggled and degrees are earned. Otherwise beers with witty names are drank from fancy glasses with his favorite person and cat.

www.ingramcontent.com/pod-product-compliance
Lightning Source LLC
LaVergne TN
LVHW041227080426
835508LV00011B/1107